# HOW TO ATTRACT WEALTH

## Your road map on how to Earn, Save, and Invest to achieve financial independence .
## ( Moving from Lack into Abundance )

Morgan Parry

# Table of contents

# Chapter 1: The Concept Of Wealth And Net Worth

## What Is Wealth?

Wealth estimates the value of all the assets of worth possessed by an individual, community, corporation, or nation. Wealth is measured by calculating the entire market worth of all physical and intangible assets held, and then deducting any obligations.

Essentially, wealth is the accumulation of limited resources.

Specific persons, companies, and countries are deemed to be affluent when they can collect numerous valuable resources or things. Wealth may be compared with income in that wealth is a stock while income is a flow, and it can be regarded in either absolute or relative terms.

*Keynotes*

- Wealth is an accumulation of valuable economic resources that may be quantified in terms of either actual products or money value.
- Net worth is the most popular measure of wealth, established by calculating the entire market value of all physical and intangible assets held and then deducting all obligations.
- The idea of wealth is normally used solely for limited economic items; assets that are plentiful and free for

everyone give no foundation for relative comparisons between persons.

- Unlike income, which is a flow variable, wealth measures the quantity of valued economic items that have been acquired at a specific moment in time.
- The relative inequalities in wealth between persons are what we normally refer to, to identify whether somebody is affluent or not.

**Understanding Wealth**

Wealth may be represented in several ways. In a strictly material sense, wealth consists of all the actual resources under one's control. Financially, net worth is the most frequent representation of wealth.

Definitions and metrics of wealth have been changed throughout time across cultures. In contemporary civilization, money is the most prevalent measure of evaluating wealth. Measuring wealth in terms of money is an illustration of money's role as a unit of account. The amount to which outside influences may affect the value of money can have a major effect on assessing wealth in this method, yet it offers a simple common denominator for comparison.

Otherwise, land and even cattle may be used to assess and evaluate wealth. In ancient times, wealth was assessed in terms of wheat, sheep, horse, or cattle held by a person.
However, with advancements in civilization and the necessity for consistency, money became a standard unit of measurement. Hence, net worth may be used as a measure of wealth and is similar across currencies. For instance, the Ancient Egyptians once judged wealth based on wheat. Herding societies have historically employed sheep, horses, or cattle as markers of prosperity.

## How to Measure Wealth

Measuring wealth in terms of money solves the challenge of evaluating wealth in the form of diverse types of things. These numbers may then be added or subtracted together. This, in turn, facilitates the practical use of net worth as a measure of wealth. Net worth is equal to assets minus liabilities. For firms, net worth is often known as shareholders' equity or book value. In common sense words, net worth describes wealth as all the actual resources under one's control, except those that ultimately belong to someone else.

Wealth is a stock variable, as opposed to a flow variable like income. Wealth defines the quantity of valued economic items gathered at a certain moment in time; income indicates the amount of money (or things) earned over a specific period.

Income reflects the increase of wealth over time (or reduction, if it is negative).

A person whose net income is positive over time will grow progressively affluent over time. For nations, gross domestic product (GDP) may be conceived of as a measure of income (a flow variable), however, it is sometimes erroneously referred to as a measure of wealth (a stock variable).
Anyone who has acquired a considerable amount of net worth might be deemed affluent, however, most people conceive of this phrase in more of a relative meaning.
Whether assessed in terms of money and net value, or commodities like wheat or sheep, overall wealth may differ across people and communities.

Research has repeatedly revealed that individuals's impressions of their well-being and pleasure rely significantly more on their assessments of wealth compared to other people than on absolute wealth. This is also part of why the idea of wealth is normally applied exclusively to limited economic items; assets that are plentiful and free for everyone give no foundation for relative comparisons between persons.

## Understanding Net Worth

A "net worth" statement or "balance sheet" is meant to present a picture of the financial stability of your organization at a certain moment in time. Net worth statements are frequently made at the beginning and closing of the accounting period (i.e. January 1) but may be done at any time.

The statement details the assets of the firm and their worth, and the liabilities or financial claims against the business (i.e. debts). The amount by which the value of the assets exceeds the liabilities is the net worth (equity) of the firm. The net worth represents the amount of ownership of the firm by the owners.

The method for determining net worth is

Assets - Liabilities = Net Worth

Likewise, the following formula helps explain the interplay of the pieces of the statement.

Assets = Liabilities + Net Worth

# *Sample balance sheet*

Assets

| | |
|---|---|
| Current | $20,000 |
| Intermediate | $80,000 |
| Long-term | $400,000 |
| Total Assets | $500,000 |

Liabilities

| | |
|---|---|
| Current | $10,000 |
| Intermediate | $60,000 |
| Long-term | $130,000 |
| Total Liabilities. | $200,000 |

Net worth $300,000

Ratios

| | |
|---|---|
| Current Ratio | 2.00 |
| Debt to Asset ratio | 0.4 |

## Classifications Of Assets and Liabilities

*Assets are frequently split into three groups;* Current or immediate, intermediate, and long-term. In certain cases, the intermediate and long-term asset categories are consolidated into one category called "fixed assets".

1. Current assets consist of cash and near-cash assets. Current assets frequently comprise assets that will be sold and converted to cash during the next accounting period. Crops and cattle kept for sale are typical current assets for a farm company.
2. Intermediate assets have a usable life of more than one year. Typical agricultural intermediate assets include machinery, equipment, and breeding cattle.
3. Long-term assets include real estate such as land, buildings, and

infrastructure. These are assets often referred to as real estate.

*Liabilities are normally categorized the same way assets are classified.*

1. Current liabilities consist of payments that are due within the next accounting period. This covers accounts payable and interest and loan payments due throughout the accounting period.

2. Intermediate liabilities consist of outstanding debt against intermediate assets and frequently have a period of three to seven years. Interest and principal payments due within the following year are included in current obligations. Only the amount of debt left after the current year's principal payment is removed is included in intermediate liabilities.

3. Long-term liabilities consist of outstanding debt against long-term assets and may have a period of 20 or more years. Interest and principal payments due within the following year on this loan are included in current liabilities. Only the amount of debt left after the current year's principal payment is removed is included in long-term liabilities.

Current assets and current liabilities offer an indicator of the cash flow of the firm for the following year. Subtracting current liabilities from current assets reveals the amount of working capital in the firm. Working capital is the amount of money utilized to enable the operations of the firm. Dividing current assets by current liabilities offers a ratio reflecting the amount of cash available per dollar of current obligations. For example, a current ratio of 2.0 suggests there is $2 in cash (or near cash assets) available for every \$1 of obligations due over the future year.

## Personal wealth

For many individuals, a long-term objective is to build and retain personal wealth for financial stability. There are many different methods to get there — savings, investments, passive income, etc. — and there are plenty of "rags to riches" success tales to inspire people's financial dreams. But there are also numerous misconceptions about money that distort the perspectives of people who aspire to obtain it. The following are some of the things you should be acquainted with while seeking to build riches.

1. Your wage isn't important; genuine riches are living off passive income.

Most individuals assume personal wealth is what you earn each year. However, it's not what you earn but what you retain and how you spend those savings. Real personal wealth is having a passive income that surpasses your costs. Buy income-generating assets with savings. True wealth is the peace of mind of knowing your living expenditures are met by the passive income you earn no matter your work situation.

## 2. Knowledge isn't enough to develop riches; you have to put it into action.

The greatest misperception for many individuals is procrastination. Personal wealth isn't just about understanding what and how. You might know what to do and how to accomplish it, but as long as you procrastinate, you are forfeiting wealth-building. Start saving. Start learning. Start paying off your debt. Just start.

**3. Your income doesn't make you rich; you have to learn how to save.**

Saving more money than you spend will make you personally rich. Would you believe there are individuals who earn $30,000 a year who have $1 million saved for retirement, and there are those who make $400,000 a year who can't figure out how to save a dollar? Don't care about what others have. Stay loyal to yourself, concentrate on your values and objectives, and live a meaningful life.

**4. Don't attempt to keep up with the Joneses; create your own healthy, personal financial objectives.**

In today's show-off world, we're overstimulated by material affluence. But bear in mind that many who represent a life of affluence are living over their means. Trying to keep up with a projected concept of someone else's financial situation will only set you up for failure. Instead, create healthy financial objectives. Another person's money will not pay your expenses and should not preoccupy your attention.

## 5. Higher returns won't always pay off; make prudent investing judgments.

Many individuals feel that striving for larger returns would yield more money in the end, but they misunderstand that higher returns come as a package deal with bigger losses when they occur. This concept of investing may lead to high fluctuation of value during the ups and downs. They fail to comprehend that the high losses degrade the accumulation worth more than big gains assist in developing value.

## 6. Wealth doesn't build immediately; you have to be patient.

Wealth is a gradual process. The media continuously promotes the lifestyles of the affluent and famous, but in fact, money is acquired slowly, over time, by being disciplined and devoted to your financial objectives. Einstein was onto something when he observed, "Compound interest is the most powerful force in the universe."

### 7. Wealth doesn't make life simpler; you have to work at retaining and expanding it.

I believe the most widespread misperception when it comes to personal wealth is that, once you're affluent, things become simpler. On the contrary, you must now pay greater attention to that riches and pay others to handle it appropriately. Just because you have it, doesn't mean you can't lose it. You have to be razor-sharp and aware of it all so you can maintain your riches and develop it.

### 8. Money is not the only thing that counts; defend your time, too.

Making a lot of money or having a lot of money is not the only thing that counts. Are you affluent if you can't afford to take a month off from work? Are you not free to pursue hobbies and interests because you are too busy attempting to enhance your wealth? I defend my time just as fiercely as I watch my bank assets.

## 9. Traditional investing isn't your sole choice; examine other avenues to retirement riches.

One of the greatest myths regarding retirement money is that you may only invest in stocks, bonds, and mutual funds. There are more possibilities than you'd expect. Alternative investments such as real estate and private equity are possible if utilizing a vehicle like a self-directed IRA. In this manner, you may grow wealth in a tax-deferred environment, investing in things you understand.

## 10. You don't need to outperform the market; keep things simple and receive solid counsel for you.

Many feel that access to elite managers who can continuously beat the markets is the method the affluent keep and grow their wealth. As it turns out, most actively managed funds underperform their benchmark over the long term and are very tax-inefficient. Minimizing taxes, obtaining solid guidance, and keeping things simple are the strategies to safeguard personal wealth for decades to come.

## The Bottom Line

The idea of wealth is subjective, primarily relying on one's view and estimate of worth. For most, money is the conventional unit of measurement, and those with an abundance of it are regarded as affluent.

There are different techniques for acquiring riches; nevertheless, there is no prescription for everyone. Despite disparities in how it is displayed, money typically gives access and opportunities that would usually be unreachable without it.

# Chapter 2: Developing a burning desire towards wealth creation

*What is a Desire for Success?*
All great accomplishment ultimately starts with an idea, but what helps ideas become reality is the fuel of human desire. A concept by itself might give you a short sensation of inspiration, but burning passion is what takes you through all the sweat required to conquer the inevitable difficulties along the road.

A burning passion for achievement is a 100% dedication to attaining the objective. It's moving from hope to knowing. It's when you want it so strongly that leaving is not an option. It's when you will do whatever it takes to attain it. You will find a way or build a way. In your imagination, you already see that objective occurring. It's a perpetual creative desire. Ask yourself now, am I genuinely pushed towards the objective that I want to achieve?

Those who have a great, burning desire to attain their objectives are sometimes referred to as being "driven." But is this exceptional trait limited just to a fortunate few? Certainly not. With the appropriate method, anybody can nurture a deep, burning desire inside themselves and advance to a level of absolute dedication, knowing with confidence that victory is as certain as the dawn.

A burning ambition is a potent motivator that motivates people toward attaining amazing achievements in business. It is the everlasting enthusiasm, commitment, and desire to succeed. Cultivating this burning passion is vital for entrepreneurs and business professionals who wish to achieve new heights.

Below are recommendations to help you spark and nurture the burning drive inside you, helping you to achieve extraordinary success in the business world.

**1. Define Your Vision:** To build a burning ambition, start by articulating a clear vision of what you want to accomplish in your company. Create a clear mental image of your objectives, desires, and the influence you wish to create. Clearly stating your goal will generate a deep emotional connection and help fuel your enthusiasm.

**2. Set Ambitious objectives:** Set tough but doable objectives that correspond with your vision. Break them down into smaller milestones to generate a feeling of progress and success. Ambitious objectives inspire and fuel your burning desire, forcing you to strive harder and go the additional mile to attain them.

**3. Fuel Your Passion:** Passion is a critical factor for building a burning drive. Identify what you are passionate about in your company and spend your attention on those areas. Surround yourself with activities, people, and resources that inspire and feed your enthusiasm. This will assist in maintaining your motivation and desire throughout hard

**4. Overcome Challenges:** Challenges and failures are inherent in the corporate environment. To create a burning passion, establish a resilient attitude that accepts mistakes as learning opportunities. View setbacks as stepping stones to development and achievement rather than roadblocks. Use setbacks to fuel your resolve and change your strategy appropriately.

### 5. Burn the Ships

If your aims are genuinely important enough to you, then you may start by burning the metaphorical ships, so that you have no alternative but to carry on. For instance, if you want to create your own company, you may begin by committing to leave your work. Write a letter of resignation, place it in a stamped envelope addressed to your employer, and send it to a trusted friend with clear instructions to mail the letter if you haven't departed your work by a specific date.

One Las Vegas casino manager chose to stop smoking. He didn't believe he had the personal fortitude to accomplish it alone, so he took a billboard on the Las Vegas Strip with his picture on it along with the slogan, "If you catch me smoking, I'll pay you $100,000!" Was he able to stop smoking? Yes! This is termed willpower leveraging. You utilize a tiny amount of willpower to generate a consequence that will nearly force you to maintain your pledge. As Andrew Carnegie famously remarked, "Put all your eggs in one basket and then watch that basket!"

In the ancient book The Art of War, Sun Tzu states that warriors battle the most furiously when they feel they're battling to the death. A competent general understands that while fighting an opposing army, it's vital to create the illusion of a possible escape path for the adversary, so they won't fight as hard. What escape routes are you leaving available that are prompting you not to fight as hard?

If you don't destroy those ships, you are giving the message to your subconscious mind that it's right to stop. And when the going gets rough, as it surely does for every great objective, you will quit. If you truly want to attain your objectives, then you've got to burn those ships to the ground and spread the ashes. If you're thinking that the typical person won't do this, you're correct - that's why they're average.

## 6. Surround Yourself with Positive People

Make friends with individuals who will support you on the road to your objectives, and find methods to spend more time with them. Share your ambitions exclusively with those who will support you, not those who will reply with cynicism or apathy. If you wish to establish a new firm, join the local chamber of commerce or a trade group. Do whatever it takes to establish new friends who will help you maintain your commitment. You'll discover that their attitudes become contagious, and you'll start thinking that you can accomplish it too.

Although this might be tough for some individuals, you also need to fire the negative people from your life. I once heard that you can glimpse your future merely by looking at the six individuals with whom you spend the most time. If you don't like what you see, then change those individuals.

There's no honor in being loyal to those who expect you to fail. One of the reasons individuals fail to establish their firms, for instance, is that they spend much of their time mingling with other workers. The way out of this trap is to start spending a lot more time networking with company owners, such as by joining a trade group. Mindsets are infectious. So spend your time with individuals whose thoughts are worth catching.

Surrounding oneself with like-minded, success-oriented folks may dramatically affect your burning ambition. Build a strong network of mentors, peers, and collaborators who inspire and drive you. Engage in mastermind groups, attend networking events, and join in communities that support your development and objectives. Their cumulative energy and success stories will keep your burning drive alive.

## 7. Embrace Continuous Learning and Empowering Information

Inspirational books and audio programs are one of the finest fuel sources for creating desire. If you want to establish a company, then start reading business literature. Attend seminars, read books and articles, listen to podcasts, and learn from mentors and successful businesses. This will continuously replenish your batteries and keep your desire impenetrably powerful.

Developing a burning passion needs a commitment to lifelong study. Stay interested, seek information, and continually endeavor to enhance your abilities and expertise. Expanding your education can not only boost your talents but also strengthen your love for your organization.

## 8. Replace Sources of Negative Energy with Positive Energy

Take an inventory of all the sensory inputs in your life that impact your attitude – what you read, what you watch on TV, the cleanliness of your house, etc. Note which inputs impact you adversely, and seek to replace them with good ones. I'll offer you some solid locations to start. First, avoid viewing energy-depleting TV news – it's largely negative. Do you need to hear about the lady who was mauled to death by her neighbor's dog? Fill that time with good stimuli instead, such as motivating and instructional audio programs. If you prefer to watch movies, then watch movies that are full of positive energy, such as light-hearted comedies and tales of victory over hardship. Avoid gloomy, sorrowful movies that leave you feeling empty afterward. Dump the scary novels, and replace them with funny literature. Spend more time smiling and less time worrying.

If you have a dirty desk, clear it up! If you have small kids or grandchildren, spend some time playing with them. Some of this may seem a little cheesy, but it will assist in raising your overall motivation. If you have a hard time motivating yourself, chances are that your life is brimming with too many sources of negativity. It's much better to gladly accomplish than it is to believe you must succeed to be happy.

## 9. Dress for Success

Whenever you pass by a mirror, which is usually numerous times a day, you receive an immediate dose of image reinforcement. So what image are you now reinforcing? Would you dress any differently if your ambitions were already achieved? Would you sport a different hairstyle? Make sure the clothing you wear each day is congruent with your new self-image.

## 10. Use Mental Programming

This is a Neuro-Linguistic Programming (NLP) strategy that can help you attach powerful positive feelings to any objective you're striving to attain. Find some music that genuinely energizes and motivates you. Put on your headphones and listen to music for fifteen to twenty minutes, and while you do this, build a clear mental image of yourself having already accomplished the outcomes you seek. Make your images huge, brilliant, vibrant, colorful, three-dimensional, panoramic, and dynamic. Picture the situation as if viewing through your own eyes (this is extremely crucial). This will help you build a neuro-association between the good feelings evoked by the music and the objective you wish to attain, thereby boosting your desire. This is a terrific way to begin each day, and you can even do it while lying in bed when you first awaken if you put things up the night before. You should cycle the music occasionally because the emotional energy you receive will likely lessen if you listen to the same songs each time.

## 11. Take Immediate And Consistent Action

Once you create a goal for yourself, act quickly. As you begin working on a fresh new objective, don't worry too much about developing precise long-term goals. Too frequently individuals become trapped in the condition of analytical paralysis and never reach the action stage. You may construct your strategy later but begin going first. Just determine the exact first physical action you need to perform, and then execute it.

Cultivating a burning passion is pointless without taking regular action. Break down your goals into concrete stages and build a disciplined routine that corresponds with your aims. Embrace the power of consistency and commit to performing tiny, meaningful acts every day. This will reinforce your burning desire, develop momentum, and push you toward your company's success.

One of the keys to success is realizing that inspiration follows action. The momentum of constant activity builds motivation, but procrastination destroys motivation. So act courageously, as if it's impossible to fail. If you keep adding gasoline to your ambition, you will reach the point of knowing that you'll never stop, and ultimate victory will be nothing more than a question of time.

Let your burning passion become the driving force behind your company's success and the key to unlocking your maximum potential towards generating riches.
If you have enough positive energy flowing into you, you'll soon have wonderful outcomes pouring out of you. And you'll

rapidly become the type of person who others refer to as "driven."

# Chapter 3: Reshaping your beliefs regarding wealth

A lot of individuals strive to become affluent but are constrained by certain limiting ideas. Your thoughts about money play a crucial part in producing riches. Some of the limiting beliefs include the following:

## 1 - I don't deserve a lot of money

Having a self-limiting notion like "I don't deserve a lot of money" might hold you back from attaining your financial objectives. This mentality will deprive you of the ability to acquire the things you desire.

The simplest method to refute this notion is to start by looking at your assets. Focus on what you have and what you want to accomplish with it. Then take the initial steps towards reaching your financial objectives.

The most essential thing to remember is that you don't have to settle for average. You have to adjust your thinking. This can be done with a little guts and determination.

You may be startled to realize that some of your views are not all that. Some of these may be hidden in your subconscious thoughts. You will need to make sure you know what's what, and follow a smart money script to get the most out of your money. This will not only help you reach your financial objectives but also drive you to success in other aspects of your life.

As you continue to make adjustments to your ideas and money practices, you will notice the difference in your life. It is easy to grow comfortable and lazy with your money, but you must do something to interrupt the loop. With a little patience and persistence, you will watch your riches increase. Moreover, you may start with tiny, verifiable successes like learning how to save more, or even how to spend your money wisely. The next time you hear the self-limiting notion, "I don't deserve a lot," replace it with an optimistic statement such as "I deserve a lot of money." It is the ideal approach to begin on your road to financial freedom.

## 2- Money is the source of all evil

Having a negative perception of money may have a very harmful influence on your life. It may keep you from accomplishing the things that you want to do and prohibit you from receiving the outcomes that you desire.

It's crucial to discover the basis of the negative thinking and get rid of it. By doing so, you may build a new reality for yourself. Then you may teach your subconscious mind to accept that new reality.

People who are caught in a negative financial position frequently have restrictive views about money. These ideas are typically founded on fear. They generate friction and anger that inhibits them from generating money.

A limiting belief about money is a conviction that you're not good enough or that you don't deserve to earn money. It's a false fact that shuts off your overflowing vitality.

The darker portions of humanity thirst for material money, power, and control. They become slaves to their money and lose sight of their integrity. This leads to the complete depravity of mankind.

To modify your limiting belief about money, you need to go to the root of the thought. This may be done by reading an affirmation or writing down an alternate belief. You may then question the limiting belief with your alternative beliefs.

You may also utilize visualization methods to get rid of the limiting thought. You may see yourself earning money and how you're going to utilize it to make a difference in the world.

Changing a limiting mindset may have a very good influence on your life. But it won't happen overnight. You'll need to know yourself well and find helpful beliefs. Then you'll need to discover methods to execute your ideas.

### 3- Money isn't going to cure all your issues

Despite all the hoopla, money isn't the solution to all your issues. If you're utilizing your money badly, you won't receive anything from it. This is particularly true if you are a large spender.

The greatest approach to utilizing your hard-earned wealth is to be a good steward. You'll get more bang for your buck if you are prepared to put in the time and work necessary to do it well. An excellent beginning point is to read up on financial planning. If you can, invest in a savings account. This will guarantee that you don't have to depend on payday loan sharks.

Although money isn't going to heal all your woes, it does come in helpful in addressing the most typical financial snafus. For example, purchasing a new automobile may be out of your grasp, but a car loan isn't. You may take out a loan and pay it off in less than two years, depending on your credit rating. This will also help you save for a property.

As with everything in life, there's more to it than purchasing a new automobile. You need to think about your lifestyle and aspirations before making any significant purchases. Aside from the most apparent ones, such as purchasing a home, you should also consider your health. By consuming nutritious food and exercising, you may enhance your overall health. This will lead to a longer and happier life.

A lot of people forget that money can't heal all your issues. You need to make a choice based on what's essential to you and your family, and then manage your money appropriately. This might imply the difference between living in a luxury and being a financial slave.

## 4- Wanting more money is greedy

Having extra money in your pocket is probably not the most joyful aspect of your day. The finest part of life is the people you are with and the possibilities you are provided with. However, the cost of products and services goes on growing every year and your wage simply won't cut it. The need for a larger buck may not be on your schedule, but it is in your best advantage to prepare ahead.

In terms of money, you'll want to follow the advice of your financial advisor. This is particularly true if you are a young professional. You should not feel compelled to take on debt to fulfill your costs. This is a karma action that will have a lasting influence on your well-being.

Although you aren't going to win any money games, there are things you can do to make the most of your hard-earned cash. For example, a side business is a terrific way to monetize your leisure time. You may make additional money by performing chores such as clearing out your desk drawers or writing reviews for local companies. The correct sort of side employment might even supply you with a second income. It's also a good idea to have a savings account. You never know when an emergency may spring up.

The most essential lesson is to be prepared for the unexpected. There are no promises that you'll receive a raise, but being prepared and equipped with an emergency fund may keep you on the right road.

## 5- Managing money is too much worry

Managing money is hard for practically everyone. If you are suffering stress due to money, you may learn to handle it by following a few steps. Financial stress may lead to emotional and physical health difficulties, and it can take a toll on your life.

Managing money is stressful, but it is not as burdensome as it may appear. The most essential thing you can do is to take a deep breath and relax. If you are having a hard time coping with your money, you may chat with a buddy who understands the problem.

This will help you put things into perspective.

Having a detailed budget might help you feel more in control of your money. Set a spending limit and make modifications if you spend more than you earn. You may also learn to manage your money in a manner that permits you to pay off your debt and save for the future.

There are numerous free resources available to learn how to handle your money. Some of these materials include books, podcasts, and newsletters. You may choose to concentrate on a particular area of your money or you can attempt to handle them all at once. Whatever strategy you select, you will find it simpler to manage your money if you build excellent habits.

The more you know about your money, the less worry you will face. You should start by noting all of your spending, including the amount you spend on your staples. It's also a good idea to have a trustworthy friend or family member tell you about their own experiences with money. Having a companion to listen to your money issues will make you more willing to deal with them.

## *How to Overcome Limiting Beliefs With Positive Self-Talk and Reframe Your Thoughts*

Getting over limiting ideas may be done using positive self-talk and reframing your thinking. You need to uncover the ideas that support your limiting beliefs and then reframe them.

### 1) Get to the bottom of your thinking

Identifying limiting beliefs is the first step to overcoming them. If you have a bad thinking about yourself, your career, your relationships, or your general mental health, it is crucial to get to the bottom of it. Once you do, you will be able to replace the previous tale with a new one.

You may begin by jotting down your ideas. You may also use a mental health tracker to help you identify when you are prompted by anxiety or other emotional states. You may then hunt for the data that supports a limiting viewpoint, or you can pick an alternative tale.

Once you recognize your limiting belief, you may write it down and evaluate a viable alternative. You may also ask other people for their opinion. This will help you understand how your beliefs are influencing your performance, relationships, and self-esteem.

Lastly, you might choose to take action against limiting ideas. When you act against a limiting notion, you will feel better about yourself. This will make you more confident in your talents, and it will lead to results. You may choose to act on your limiting belief alone, or you can have a friend or a family member support you.

The process of recognizing limiting beliefs may be hard. You may need to visit a counselor. Technology has made it simpler to locate a therapist. You may also call a therapist over a cell phone.

It might be tough to break away from limiting ideas, but with effort, you can learn how to detect them and alter them. Doing so will allow you to build confidence, strengthen your relationships, and move on in your life.

It's crucial to identify a limiting mindset since it might impair your capacity to attain your objectives. The next time you're thinking of a negative idea, try to think of a good example.

## 2) Reframe your ideas

Trying to reframe your thinking might help you develop a better understanding of your emotions. Negative ideas may lead to unpleasant sensations, and they can restrict your life. But with the appropriate procedure, they can be transformed.

Reframing may be a tough process, but it can also be rewarding. It might be a method to transform your perspective and start forging a new path for yourself.

To get started, you need to recognize your limiting beliefs. You may achieve this by maintaining a thinking diary. You may also communicate with others and ask for comments. These approaches will help you define what your limiting beliefs are, and how to overcome them.

You may also attempt reframing by speaking positive affirmations out loud. These are proven to help educate your mind to perceive things differently. By doing this, you will begin to convert your negative ideas into good ones.

It's vital to bear in mind that reframing is not about pretending everything is fine. It's about taking your actions in a new manner and shifting the meaning of occurrences.

It's also crucial to remember that reframing may become a habit, so you will need to practice consistently to make it a constant part of your life. You may evaluate your reframed beliefs regularly, and construct a chart to keep track of them. This chart may be read before you start your day, and before you go to sleep at night.

Reframing your thinking is a process that might take some work, but it can be worth it. With the aid of this strategy, you may start to break free from your restricting habits and become a more resourceful, confident, and healthy self.

### 3) Positive self-talk

Using positive self-talk may be an excellent strategy to overcome limiting thoughts. Some individuals have a tough time getting rid of their negative self-talk. This sort of thinking might impede children from being happy and healthy. However, with sufficient work, you can change those negative ideas into constructive energy.

A smart place to start is to think about what your limiting beliefs are. For instance, if you have a limiting view that you can't be excellent at anything, you may be afraid to attempt new activities, even if they may enhance your life. Instead, you need to come up with a plan to challenge this notion.

One of the greatest methods to do this is to write down your limiting beliefs. Not only will this help you comprehend your negative ideas, but it will also assist you to discover their source. You may also utilize an audio program to inform you when your self-limiting beliefs are ready to pop up.

Another successful strategy is to write out a list of topics you are interested in, and then concentrate on one item a day. This will assist you in attaining greater attention. For example, if you have a desire to obtain more exercise, you may want to jot down activities you like doing, such as walking, hiking, or swimming. This will help you remember to do them.

Finally, you might make use of a mantra, or affirmation, to assist you in getting back on track. A mantra is an effective self-talk tactic because it puts you in the appropriate state of mind. You may also practice your mantra regularly to keep yourself motivated.

Although it's not usually the simplest thing to do, utilizing positive self-talk to assist you in overcoming your limiting beliefs may help you attain your objectives.

### 4) Identify ideas that promote a limiting belief

Identifying ideas that support a limiting belief might assist you in overcoming the limiting beliefs you may have been holding. These limiting ideas might be keeping you from realizing your actual potential. They may also impair your physical health and family ties.

Oftentimes, limiting beliefs are generated from an idea or an opinion. These views might be a consequence of a person's experiences or a lack of confidence. They may also be a consequence of untruth. They may also be a defensive mechanism that keeps you safe from short-term or long-term discomfort. Getting rid of limiting ideas is achievable, but it needs self-awareness and a shift of viewpoint.

The greatest technique to discover a limiting belief is to write down your ideas. You should strive to determine what is the limiting belief, what is the purpose of the limiting belief, and what are your intended objectives. Then, you might attempt to replace the limiting mindset with an empowering one.

Another effective technique to detect a limiting mindset is by evaluating your history. You should ask yourself why you have had terrible experiences and what was the greatest result you were able to accomplish from those events. You should then take that information and apply it to your present life.

You may also use a mental health tracker to help you monitor your emotional condition. This can give you a better view of the triggers that keep you feeling worried or nervous. You should next strive to locate data that opposes your limiting beliefs.

If you have a tough time breaking limiting beliefs, you should seek expert treatment. A therapist can assist you with this process. You may also call a counselor on your cell phone.

### 5)Push beyond limiting beliefs

Identifying and pushing beyond limiting ideas is a key element of personal growth and leadership. They may inhibit personal progress and prohibit individuals from obtaining success in their lives.

When limiting beliefs are discovered and addressed, they may be converted into positive beliefs. If you have a limiting notion about working in a white-collar job, you might opt to pursue a profession in which you are enthusiastic.

If you hold a restricting mindset about finding love, you may replace the limiting thinking with a more empowered one. If you have a limiting notion that there aren't enough Italian restaurants in the world, you may reframe your thinking and say, "There are plenty of Italian restaurants in the world. I'll start hunting for them."

If you have a limiting idea that you won't make it to the top of your firm, you may begin to confront it. You may chat with a counselor using a mobile phone, or you can acquire a mental health tracker to help you monitor your feelings and your progress.

Limiting beliefs aren't always straightforward to detect. They might be triggered by experiences in your history. For example, if you observe a role model fail and you laugh at it, you may develop a limiting mindset that you won't succeed.

You might also have restricting views about your family or friends. If you have a limiting belief, you will likely not be able to have constructive confrontations with them. They may feel intimidated by your adjustments.

You may challenge limiting beliefs by writing them down and assessing the influence of them on your life. You may find them in the way you connect with your family or in your money.

# Chapter 4: The power of affirmations

Using subconscious mind-affirmations that are created particularly for the subconscious mind is a very simple technique to reach the subconscious mind and train it for riches.

The reality is that affirmations have been around for quite some time and a lot of people have been doing it. But, of all the folks who have been affirming one thing or the other, they've discovered that they find it difficult to actualize what they are affirming every day.

Contrary to what you may have thought about affirmations, I'm here to inform you that affirmations do work (when done appropriately) when you are attempting to reach your subconscious mind.

I will let you know why it doesn't work for most people and how you would do it differently so that you can start manifesting whatever it is you want to create.

Firstly, what are positive affirmations?
Positive affirmations are positive comments that confirm something to be true. The premise behind affirmations is that when a positive attitude towards life is backed with affirmations, success in everything may be reached.

If this is the premise, why is it difficult for a lot of individuals to materialize the good things they desire in their lives using positive affirmations?
Why is it that a lot of individuals typically materialize what they do not desire instead?
The answer to these questions is that one way or the other; everyone utilizes affirmations every day of our lives. The distinctions are that some people use it

purposefully and positively, while other people use it mistakenly, unwittingly, and badly.

We all say one thing or the other during our day. Some individuals are in the habit of letting their lips run off and they start confirming things they don't want in their life.
As gradual as it may be, ultimately, things you say and believe will reach your subconscious mind. And your subconscious mind will start making your life's choices based on these ideas.

The function of the subconscious mind when it comes to positive affirmations is that the subconscious mind is the home of your beliefs and your behaviors.

Until your subconscious mind accepts what you are affirming as reality, there will be no apparent benefits from your affirmations.

This is where a lot of folks get affirmations incorrect. They keep speaking one thing, but their subconscious mind thinks something another.

The subconscious mind is incredibly crucial to generating anything you desire. If you want to hack your subconscious mind to believe an affirmation quicker, here are three vital actions to tick off your list;

*1.Visualize when you are affirming*

The subconscious mind can only be communicated with by the use of mental pictures.

Images are a kind of language that the subconscious mind knows.

If your affirmations are not coupled with any type of visual, they are simply words.

It is till you start connecting pictures with your affirmations that it begins getting powerful. At this level, the visuals will be emotionalizing what you are confirming.

The techniques to achieve this successfully are;

- By utilizing vision boards with your affirmations.

Get images of anything you wish to confirm. For instance, if your affirmation is "I vacation every summer in exotic locations all around the world", pick a magazine that includes photographs of places you would want to travel and cut the picture out. Attach this photo to a board and write your affirmation plainly beneath.

When you are ready to utilize the affirmation, gaze at the graphics on the board while uttering the words. See yourself at that spot in your mind's eye enjoying a wonderful time there.

- By utilizing custom-made affirmation cards that are produced with pictures of those affirmations that you carry about.

These days, some affirmation cards come with photos in the backdrop.

These graphics are connected to the affirmation message on the cards.

So that when you wish to say the affirmation and glance at the card, the visuals stimulate your creative brain. This makes it simpler to visualize yourself in your mind's eye present in the situation you are attempting to affirm.

- By utilizing your mind's eye directly.

This may either be done manually or in a guided way.

The manual form is that as you are reading the affirmations, you start envisioning yourself as the person who possesses whatever it is you are affirming.

In the manual method, you may apply the use of previous memories or use someone you know either in real life, on TV, or via a book you read that includes what you want to confirm as a point of reference.

For instance, if you are confirming being a confident person, you may envision a moment in the past when you've been confident. If it is not accessible, you might imagine becoming someone you know who is a confident person and putting yourself in their place while you are chanting the affirmation.

*2. Igniting your inventive brain via the guided form.*

This is by far the most effective way of forming distinct mental pictures.

This may be done by having affirmations that have binaural beats playing underneath—which assists you in going to the alpha brainwave state quicker.

The availability of a tranquil voice bringing you to visualization, while reading the positive affirmations to you in this alpha state makes this approach more potent and incredibly successful.

*3.Focus on some select sets of affirmations.*

Here is where some individuals shoot themselves in the foot when it comes to affirmations;
They simply wander about and never concentrate. Some folks chant two hundred different affirmations in a day.
This way, nothing will stick. Make sure you concentrate on one aspect of your life you desire to enhance and start utilizing two to three affirmations that will actualize them.
When you feel like you are finished with those, that is, you've experienced the

tangible consequences in your life, then, you may pick up another area and concentrate on them.

### Repetition is crucial

When it comes to positive affirmations for the subconscious mind, everyday repetition is key.

When you are practicing affirmations appropriately, that is, linking mental pictures with your affirmations, the only thing left to do is to repeat it regularly.

This is the technique that the quickest results may be acquired. Even better, do it twice or thrice every day.

The reason for this is that the negative ideas in your subconscious mind were not established over only a month. They were progressively placed throughout your life, until today.

So, to alter it back via affirmations won't happen quickly. It will take some time and consistent practice for it to reverse.

# Chapter 5: Reasons You Should Be Wealthy

There are various reasons why one might desire to become affluent. It includes the following:

## Financial independence

Attaining financial independence is an ambition for most folks. Financial independence typically means having enough savings, financial assets, and cash on hand to finance the sort of life we wish for ourselves and our families. It implies accumulating funds that allow us to retire or follow the job we desire without being motivated by earning a specific wage each year. Financial independence implies our money is working for us rather than the other way around.

To become financially free, you must pay off your consumer debts, construct a safety net of savings money, and earn enough passive income via investment or company ownership to compensate for your present and predicted future living needs.

We are plagued with mounting debt, monetary crises, excessive consumer spending, and other obstacles that prohibit us from accomplishing our most significant financial aspirations. Such obstacles affect anyone, but the following twelve behaviors may set you on the optimal route to financial well-being.

## Purpose and Fulfillment

In today's world, it's easy to become caught up in the desire for money. However, relying primarily on financial achievement might lead to a lack of purpose in life. True fulfillment comes from finding purpose and significance beyond monetary aspirations. By recognizing our identity, beliefs, and interests, we may design a life that is satisfying and effective.

The desire for money may lead to a sense of emptiness and lack of satisfaction. While it's crucial to be financially comfortable, it's also important to concentrate on finding meaning beyond monetary achievement. Fulfillment comes from living a life that resonates with our beliefs, interests, and ambitions. Here are some methods to achieve meaning and satisfaction in life beyond financial success:

*Identify Your Passions and Use Them to Create a Life Goal* .
Take time to focus on your hobbies and interests. What inspires you and provides you joy? Once you've recognized your passion, utilize it to establish a life goal. For example, if you're enthusiastic about the environment, you might establish a goal to decrease your carbon footprint and support

eco-friendly efforts. By matching your monetary objectives with your passion, you can guarantee that your money is going towards something that matters to you.

*Focus on Your Values*
Values are what we care about strongly and attempt to keep in our lives. They might be anything from being nice to others to pursuing social justice. By concentrating on your principles, you may make a good influence in the world and lead a life of meaning. For example, if your value is to assist people in need, you may volunteer at a local charity or contribute money to a nonprofit that helps those in need.

*Embrace Your Identity*
We all have numerous components of our identity, and it's crucial to identify and appreciate these sides of ourselves. By doing so, we may construct an identity that is more than just one item and that offers a

feeling of purpose and meaning. For example, if you define yourself by your profession, it's crucial to know that you're more than simply your job title. Embrace your various identities, such as being a parent, friend, or community member.

*Create a Lasting Legacy*
What type of effect do you want to create on the world? What do you want to be known for? By leveraging your abilities, resources, and interests, you can make a lasting change in the world. You may establish a company that promotes social issues, form a charity that assists people in need or utilize your abilities to develop something that benefits future generations.

In conclusion, although it's necessary to be financially secure, it's also crucial to discover purpose and meaning beyond monetary achievement. By defining our interests, values, and identities, we may construct a life that is rewarding and effective. When we concentrate on finding purpose beyond money, we may lead a life that is replete with meaning, pleasure, and satisfaction.

## Financial Security

From a nuts and bolts standpoint, being financially secure implies that you're financially equipped to withstand unanticipated crises or adversities; and that you can sustain a comfortable lifestyle on an ongoing basis. It implies that your needs and desires are covered—although not necessarily permanently (that would indicate you're financially independent, which is similar but distinct), and you have the skills and resources to keep up with those needs and wants.

Depending on the era of life you're in, what constitutes financial security or the conditions to having attained it might alter.

For example, if you're just starting, financial stability may be as easy as having a budget, a thorough knowledge of your cash flow, and being in a position where you can develop an emergency fund. For young people, financial stability also frequently means turning human capital into financial capital in the form of a job that provides you money. As a consequence, financial stability for a young individual may look like accumulating their first $1,000 in a savings account, having positive cash flow, and managing their debt.

In contrast, financial stability bears different connotations for retired individuals. Instead of fulfilling their requirements and goals with earned money from a job, additional sources of income like pension plans and investments must be able to assist them in doing that—and these resources are likely to endure their lifetime. Ultimately, it still boils down to having financial stability, power, and freedom.

Can anybody ever genuinely be financially secure?
Financial stability isn't an end point—rather, it's a way of being. It alludes to the effort on an individual's side to develop an awareness of their financial condition and take action to have control over their circumstances.

While you may obtain a feeling of financial security, it's a never-ending path in that, after you've done so, you must preserve it. Some individuals have financial systems in place that would take a lot to endanger, but it might still happen. This is why smart money management and risk management are crucial to not only becoming but being, financially secure.
As with many things in life, it's about the journey—not the goal!

*How Financial Security Affects Your Family* .

Having a sense of financial security and control may produce a powerful sensation of independence. Evidence demonstrates that being financially stable also decreases stress and anxiety, which is incredibly advantageous to everyone within a family dynamic. It may even increase your confidence.

When you're financially secure, this provides you the ability to concentrate on other elements of your life since you won't constantly be thinking about money. This is why knowing your financial condition is vital. If you're focusing on making ends meet, it will penetrate every facet of your life. Knowledge is the first step to take control.

Financial stability might also empower you to make better judgments. It puts you in a situation where you've got yourself covered, so you can start concentrating on helping others. (Think of it like an airline oxygen mask). This means you'll have the time, energy, and cash to examine your family's financial goals and even charity aims.

Since financial security and financial independence are distinct, it may not mean that you're flying first class twice a year, but your life will still be secure and meaningful. You may also transform financial stability into financial opportunity by utilizing debt to grow wealth or via other ways.

*How And When To Use Debt To Build Wealth*
If you've created financial stability, and you have a solid status as well as a strong awareness of your circumstances, you may wish to approach the notion of utilizing debt

to grow wealth. This might include purchasing real land or acquiring a commercial loan for your firm. Whether this is the appropriate choice for you boils down to risk management. You could analyze the risk and determine that the technique of utilizing debt to create wealth does match your lifestyle, and if your plan doesn't work out, you'll still have the financial means to get by.

Part of analyzing risk entails ensuring that you won't get overleveraged (i.e., that you won't take on more debt than your cash flow can support). This is where individuals may get into difficulty and compromise their financial stability. Sometimes, things go south with the usage of debt, and people can't pay their commitments, which undermines all of the work they've done thus far to develop wealth and financial stability. Working with a financial adviser to obtain a strong grasp of your circumstances may assist you in preventing this from occurring to you. The trick is to put your financial stability above all else and acquire an eye for risk management.

*How To Turn Financial Security Into Financial Opportunity*

Financial stability is the basis upon which you may explore additional alternatives and begin to utilize your financial resources in new ways. You can consider investing your extra wealth in the stock market, establishing a company, or going back to school and gaining the skills to begin a new job. Or, you could be getting set to retire and follow your hobbies and charity aspirations at a new level.

# Chapter 6: Goals Setting And Projecting Yourself For Wealth Creation

## *How To Set Clear And Realistic Goals*

Setting realistic financial objectives is a critical step toward attaining financial stability and long-term success. Whether your objectives entail saving for a down payment on a house, paying off debt, or creating an emergency fund, having a clear strategy in place boosts your chances of success.

Following these suggestions can help you attain your goals:

Review your financial condition

Before creating financial objectives, it is vital to examine your existing financial situation. Take stock of your income, spending, debts, and savings. Analyze your spending patterns and discover areas where you might make adjustments. Understanding your financial boundaries helps in developing realistic objectives that correspond with your resources.

## Define your priorities

Identify your short-term and long-term financial priorities. Do you wish to pay off high-interest debt, invest for retirement, or establish a business? Prioritize your objectives based on their relevance and urgency. This will help you organize your resources wisely and concentrate your attention on what matters most to you.
Break down major ambitions into smaller milestones

Large financial objectives might be daunting. Break them down into smaller milestones. For instance, if you aim to pay off a considerable amount of debt, create monthly or quarterly milestones to measure your progress. Celebrating these tiny triumphs along the road can keep you motivated and make the greater objective more accessible.

## Be practical and time-bound

Set objectives that are reasonable and feasible depending on your present financial status. While it's vital to dream large, establishing unattainable objectives may lead to frustration and disappointment. Consider aspects including your income, spending, and savings capacity. Attach particular time boundaries to your objectives to generate a feeling of urgency and responsibility.

## Increase your savings

Set precise and well-defined objectives that are explicit and quantifiable. For example, instead of stating, "I want to save more," state how much you want to save and by when.

With time, age, and work experience, your income will rise. Do not save at 40 as you did at 25. Make your greater discretionary money work for you. If you are saving 10% of your salary today, aim towards attaining 20% and from there, 30%. Stepping up your savings can help you accomplish your financial objectives faster."

## Save Money For Your Financial Goals

Break down each objective into manageable tasks and establish timeframes for fulfilling them. Whether it entails raising your income, lowering costs, or obtaining expert assistance, a well-structured action plan helps keep you on track and guarantees you are making progress.

## Monitor your financial activities

Regularly examine and analyze your progress toward your financial objectives. Whether it entails raising your income, lowering costs, or obtaining expert assistance, a well-structured action plan helps keep you on track and guarantees you are making progress. Keep track of your income, spending, savings, and debt reduction. Use tools like budgeting apps or spreadsheets to track your financial actions. Regular check-ins will help you to make modifications, discover areas for growth, and remain inspired as you watch your progress unfold.

**Seek Support**

Sharing your objectives with someone who can give support, guidance, or keep you accountable may be good. Whether it's a friend, family member, or a financial adviser, having someone to share your path with may drive you.

## Stay flexible

Life is unpredictable, and financial situations might change. Stay adaptable and be prepared to alter your objectives as required. Unexpected costs or changes in revenue may compel you to adapt your schedule or rethink your methods. Embrace the necessity for flexibility and be open to making required alterations along the road.

## Reward Yourself

It is time to rejoice. When you attain a financial milestone or reach a goal, celebrate your achievement. Rewarding yourself, within reason, for your hard work and devotion helps.

Take stock of your income, spending, obligations, and savings first

Set objectives that are reasonable and feasible depending on your present financial condition.

Regularly monitor and analyze your progress toward your financial objectives.

Be open to making required alterations along the way.

## Setting Yourself Up To Attract Wealth

The Law of Attraction is the notion that we can attract whatever we are concentrating on, from prosperity to love and happiness. This approach altered my life, but it doesn't work for everyone. That's because many people forget the other half of the equation: Attracting what you desire isn't enough; you also need to take action.

Here are eight practical strategies to set you up for wealth:

### 1. Face your fears.

To become successful, you must conquer your fears. Some individuals dread failure; others fear success. Many are terrified of making the incorrect choice and don't make one at all. It's easy to imagine that you can always start tomorrow – but genuine failure is never having tried.

Rather than dread the inevitable problems, what if you were only to accept that they are part of life? Problems are only conditions that precede answers and opportunities.

## 2. Create reminders everywhere.

The Law of Attraction promotes speaking affirmations and envisioning yourself obtaining your objectives. As explained before, employing the phrase "I am" talks straight to your subconscious. Write down your objectives and affirmations; print photographs of what you're aiming for and post them around your house and business. When you see them regularly, it further imprints them in your memory.

Visualization is most effective when supported by strong, happy emotions. Imagine how it will feel to attain your objectives. That's what will inspire you.

### 3. Execute huge ideas.

Taking action involves putting in the effort and getting started on your ideas. When you have a huge idea, write it down while you're inspired. Then describe immediate measures you can take to make it true. It may be researching to see whether it's realistic, or informing a buddy so you have some responsibility.

### 4. Mimic others.

To be the greatest at what you do, just adopt what your rivals do – then do it better or differently. Study their websites and marketing materials. Strive to be the sort of firm where their finest individuals want to work. I've discovered several tactics via employing individuals from rivals.

Mentors are also vital, but they don't need to be pricey leadership trainers. A mentor might be an author whose words inspire you or an influencer with encouraging YouTube videos.

## 5. Exercise.

Your physical health affects all parts of your life. You undoubtedly know you should exercise — but do you permit yourself to do it on your terms? For example, if you aren't a morning person, don't work out in the morning. If you despise the gym, try a team sport or walk home from work.

It's simple to cut out exercise to save time throughout the day, but don't. Going for a 15-minute stroll is considerably better than not doing anything at all.

Use exercise as a tool to fulfill other objectives, including spending time alone, which is crucial for success. The greatest breakthroughs occur alone, so take time for yourself every day.

## 6. Give with emotion.

If you want to receive, you have to give. This doesn't only pertain to money; there's another layer. I call it vibrational giving.

Focus on the feeling you experience when donating. When you contribute money and feel good about it, you will get something in return with a positive emotion attached. It may be money, but it might not.

When you tell someone to have a nice day, don't say it mechanically. Mean it and feel love behind that wish, and you'll receive it in return.

This is another reason the Law of Attraction doesn't work for everyone. Don't donate only to obtain anything in return. Don't offer money to someone in need and expect them to utilize it in a specific manner. Help them because you know the delight it will provide them.

## 7. Invest in your team.

To be the greatest, you have to work with the best – and pay them what they're worth. This investment doesn't have to be money. Build a "once-in-a-lifetime" culture. Offer advantages like education or wellness initiatives. Create tiny moments of enjoyment by organizing a special lunch for your staff or shutting the office early on a Friday. Give workers ownership and trust. It's much simpler to be successful with a great team behind you.

Celebrate large and little accomplishments as a team. By applauding success, you might establish an addiction to it.

### 8. Enjoy it and keep it up.

Wealth isn't only about money. It's also about having free time to appreciate it and separate from work. Learn to appreciate moments with loved ones without being psychologically tethered to your business.

For long-term riches, you must maintain the habits that made you successful in the first place, even when the going gets rough.

When things began going wrong with my first company, I let fear get the better of me. I dreaded what would happen if I lost all I'd fought so hard for. My imagination moved to a world of poverty rather than plenty. I stopped making time to create objectives, envision, and keep active, and that company finally collapsed. When I renewed all these routines, it didn't take long to reclaim my success.

**Stay cheerful and refuse to surround yourself with negativity.**

If I find myself amid a gossip-filled or nasty discussion, I excuse myself to the toilet or pretend I have a phone call. If you can govern your thinking, you can control your life.

# Chapter 7: Fundamentals of wealth creation

Building money is a goal that many individuals aspire to, yet it can sometimes feel like an onerous endeavor. It takes time, work, and discipline to be successful with this aim, so don't be misled by get-rich-quick schemes and too-good-to-be-true offers that might lead you down a perilous road.

The good news is that some ideas and practices may help anybody grow and keep money in the long run. And, the sooner you start putting things into practice, the higher your odds of success.

Below, are details of some fundamental ideas for generating wealth, including establishing objectives and forming a strategy, investing in education and skills, managing debt, saving and investing, safeguarding your assets, recognizing the effect of taxes, and having a great credit history.

We will take a deeper look at each of these concepts and how they might help you reach your financial objectives.

*Basic steps*

Building wealth over time is a question of following three fundamental actions and adhering to them.

- The first stage is to generate enough money to satisfy your necessities, with some surplus for saving.
- The second stage is to control your expenditure so that you may maximize your savings.
- The third stage is to put your money in several different assets so that it's appropriately diversified for the long run.

## 1. Earn Money

The first thing you need to do is start producing money. This step may appear basic but is the most essential one for individuals who are just beginning out. You've certainly seen charts indicating that a small amount of money routinely saved and allowed to compound over time ultimately may develop into a large sum. But such charts never address this fundamental question: How do you earn money to save in the first place?

There are two fundamental methods of producing money: via earned revenue or passive income. Earned money originates from what you do for a livelihood, whereas passive income is earned from assets. You may not have any passive income until you've acquired enough money to begin investing.

If you are either about to start a profession or considering a career shift, these questions may help you decide on what you want to do—and where your earned money is going to come from:

*What do you enjoy?* You will perform better, develop a longer-lasting career, and be more likely to succeed financially by doing something that you like and find significant. One research revealed that more than nine out of 10 workers stated they would sacrifice a proportion of their career earnings for more meaning at work.

*What are you excellent at?* Look at what you do well and how you may utilize your abilities to make a livelihood.
What will pay well? Look at occupations employing what you like and perform well that will satisfy your financial aspirations.

*How do you get there?* Learn about the education, training, and experience requirements required to pursue your selected career possibilities. Taking these aspects into account might help set you on the correct road.

An excellent method to enhance your earning potential is to invest in your education and talents. Getting higher academic degrees, industry-specific certifications, and training programs are all beneficial to enhance your human capital.

## 2. Save Money

Simply producing money won't help you grow wealth if you end up spending it all. Moreover, if you don't have enough money saved up for your near-term commitments (such as bills, rent, or mortgage) or an emergency, then you should prioritize saving enough above everything else. Many experts advocate having several months' (e.g., three to six) worth of salary saved up for such occasions.

To lay more money away for developing wealth, consider these moves:

*Track your expenditures for at least a month.*
You may wish to utilize a financial software program to assist you in accomplishing this, but a compact, pocket-size notepad might also suffice. Record your every expense, no matter how tiny; many individuals are startled to find where all their money goes.

*Find the fat and trim it.*
Break down your expenses into necessities and desires. Food, shelter, and clothes are obvious requirements. Add health insurance premiums to that list, along with vehicle insurance if you own a car and life insurance if other people are depending on your income. Many other expenses will only be desires.

*Set a savings goal.*
Once you have a realistic sense of how much money you can put away each month,

attempt to keep to it. This doesn't imply that you have to live like a miser or be thrifty all the time. If you're hitting your savings objectives, feel free to treat yourself and indulge (a reasonable amount) once in a while. You'll feel better and be driven to continue on track.

*Put saving on automatic.*
One straightforward approach to saving a predetermined amount each month is to arrange with your company or bank to automatically deposit a particular percentage of every paycheck into a separate savings or investing account. Similarly, you may save for retirement by having money routinely removed from your income and deposited into other accounts as savings.

*Find high-yield savings.*
Maximize the payback of your investment by looking for savings accounts that offer the best interest rates and lowest fees. Keep this

in mind, too: You can only eliminate so much in expenses. If your expenses are already down to the bone, then you should look at methods to enhance your revenue.

One of the greatest methods to make sure you are saving enough is to create a spending budget. Cut down on excess and unneeded expenditures, and put that money in the bank instead.

## 3. Invest

Once you've managed to save some money, the next step is investing it so that it can increase. Money deposited in savings is crucial, but the interest rates credited on deposit accounts tend to be quite low, and your cash risks losing buying power over time to inflation.

Perhaps the most crucial investing principle for novices (or any investor, for that matter) is diversity. Simply said, your objective should be to disperse your money across several sorts of assets. That's because investments perform differently at various periods. For example, if the stock market is on a losing trend, bonds may be offering strong returns.

Or if Stock A is in a downturn, Stock B may be on a tear.

Mutual funds offer some built-in diversification since they invest in many different assets. And you'll obtain better diversity if you invest in both a stock fund and a bond fund (or many stock funds and several bond funds), for example, rather than in just one or the other.

As another general guideline, the younger you are, the more risk you can afford to take since you'll have more years to make up for any losses.

## Types of Investments

Investments differ in terms of risk and possible return. As a general rule, the safer they are, the lower their prospective return, and vice versa.

If you aren't already aware of the different sorts of investments, it's worth spending a little time reading up on them. While there are all sorts of exotic investments, most individuals will want to start with the basics: stocks, bonds, and mutual funds.

**Stocks** are shares of ownership in a firm. When you acquire stock, you own a little chunk of that firm and will profit from any growth in its share price, as well as any dividends that it pays out. Stocks are often viewed as riskier than bonds, although stocks may also vary substantially in risk from one firm to another.

**Bonds** are like IOUs from a firm or government. When you purchase a bond, the issuer agrees to pay your money back, with interest, after a specific term. As a very general rule, bonds are regarded as less risky than equities, but with less potential upside. At the same time, certain bonds are riskier than others; bond-rating organizations issue them letter ratings to reflect that.

**Mutual funds** are pools of securities—often stocks, bonds, or a mix of the two. When you acquire mutual fund shares, you receive a portion of the total pool. Mutual funds also vary in risk, depending on what they invest in.

Also, exchange-traded funds (ETFs) are like mutual funds in that each share contains a whole portfolio of assets, but ETFs are listed on exchanges and trade like stocks. Some ETFs follow large stock indexes like the S&P 500, individual industrial sectors, or asset classes like bonds and real estate.
Before you start investing, make sure you have adequate savings and enough money

left away to manage any unforeseen financial problems.

## 4. Protect Your Assets

You've worked hard to earn your money and expand your fortune. The worst thing may be to lose it all due to a sudden catastrophe or unanticipated incident. A fire may burn down your property, a vehicle accident can cause damage and medical expenditures, or a premature death might mean a loss of future income.

Insurance is a critical aspect of increasing your wealth since it offers protection against these and other threats. Home insurance will replace your home and valuables in case of a fire, vehicle insurance will make you whole after a car accident, and life insurance will give your dependents a death benefit in the event of an early death.

Long-term disability insurance is another form of coverage that will replace your income if you become wounded, sick, or otherwise incompetent and unable to continue working. Even young, healthy individuals should consider insurance goods as they tend to become more costly as you become older. That means that if you are 25 years old and unmarried, obtaining life insurance might be a lot more cost-effective than when you are 10 years older with a spouse, children, and mortgage.

## 5. Minimize the Impact of Taxes

Taxes are an often-overlooked burden on your wealth-building efforts. Of course, we are all liable to income tax and sales tax as we earn and spend money, but our investments and assets may also be taxed. That's why it is crucial to understand your tax risks and adopt methods to reduce their effect.

One straightforward approach to lower your tax payment is to invest in tax-advantaged accounts. These accounts, such as 529 college savings programs, individual retirement accounts (IRAs), and 401(k) plans, provide tax incentives that may help you save more money and minimize your tax burden. For example, donations to a conventional IRA or 401(k) are tax-deductible, meaning that you may lower your taxable income and save money on taxes in the year that you contribute.

Moreover, they grow tax-deferred, meaning that when you retire and are more likely to be at a lower tax rate, the effect will be reduced. Investment gains in a Roth IRA or Roth 401(k) are tax-free, meaning that you may grow and remove money in a Roth account without paying taxes on any of the income or gains.

Another technique for lowering taxes is to be conscious of the time and location of your assets. By keeping assets for more than a year, you may take advantage of the reduced long-term capital gains tax rate, which is normally lower than the short-term capital gains tax and income tax rates.

You should also be careful of where certain assets are housed. Given the option, an income-producing asset like a dividend-paying stock or corporate bond should be put in a tax-advantaged account like a Roth IRA, where these payments will not generate taxable events. A growth stock that will solely create capital gains (rather than income) could alternatively be better put in a taxable account.

Working with a skilled tax expert, such as an accountant or a certified public accountant (CPA), may help you keep on top of these developments and establish a tax plan that works for your financial circumstances. By understanding the impact of taxes and implementing ways to reduce their impact, you may create wealth more efficiently and save more of your hard-earned money over the long run.

### 6. Manage Debt and Build Your Credit

As you gain money, you'll start to find it desirable to take on debt to support certain purchases or investments. You may pay for products using a credit card to gain points or prizes. You may apply for a mortgage for a house or second home, a home equity loan for home upgrades, or an auto loan to buy a vehicle. Maybe you'll want to take out a personal loan to help establish a company or invest in someone else's.

However, it's vital to manage your debt carefully—taking on too much debt might impair your progress toward your wealth-building objectives. To manage debt, be careful of your debt-to-income (DTI) ratio and make sure that your debt payments are doable within your budget.

You should also attempt to pay off high-interest debt, such as credit card debt, as fast as possible to avoid incurring exorbitant interest costs. Be aware of variable or adjustable interest rate products like adjustable-rate mortgages (ARMs), or those with balloon payments, since changes to the economy or your circumstances may rapidly lead such loans to become unmanageable.

Indeed, if you go into debt, your credit score may be badly damaged, and if you fail on your obligations, you might risk personal bankruptcy.

## 7. Maintaining a Good Credit Score

Building and keeping a strong credit score is a vital aspect of building and safeguarding your money over the long run. You'll enjoy a reduced interest rate and better conditions on your loans if you have a great credit history and high credit score, which may save you hundreds of dollars in interest costs over time.

Here are a few crucial things that you may do to keep a decent credit score:

*Pay your bills on time.* One of the most crucial elements that impact your credit score is your payment history. To keep a decent credit score, you should be sure to pay your payments on time, every time. Late payments, even if they're just a few days late, may have a big negative influence on your credit score.
*Keep your credit use low.*
Your credit usage, or the amount of credit you're using relative to the amount you have available, is another crucial element that influences your credit score. To maintain a decent credit score, you should attempt to

keep your credit use below 30% of your available credit.

*Monitor your credit report.* It's a good idea to check your credit report often to make sure that all the information is correct and up to date. Today, various firms can offer you a credit report free of charge. Errors in your credit report may severely affect your credit score, so it's crucial to challenge any inconsistencies you notice.

*Avoid opening too many new accounts.* Every time you seek credit, it might have a slight negative influence on your credit score. To keep a decent credit score, you should avoid creating too many new accounts in a short period. Note, however, that if you do not use credit cards or don't have enough credit lines open, you may fall prey to not having an adequate credit history. So, get some credit cards and take out some loans, but do not overdo it.

By following these procedures and exercising excellent credit practices, you may maintain a strong credit score and optimize your borrowing ability over the long run.

*Should I pay off the debt or invest?*
If you have high-interest debt, such as several credit card charges, it typically makes sense to pay it off before you invest. Few investments ever pay as much as credit cards charge. Once you've paid off your debt, put that additional money into savings and investments. And attempt to pay your credit card debt in full each month, wherever feasible, to prevent paying interest in the future.

*How much money do I need to acquire a mutual fund?*
Mutual fund providers have varied minimum initial investment requirements to get started, commonly starting at roughly

$500. After that, you may typically spend less. Some mutual funds may waive their initial minimums if you agree to invest a consistent quantity each month. You may also acquire mutual fund and exchange-traded fund (ETF) shares via a brokerage business, some of which charge nothing for establishing an account.

*What is an exchange-traded fund (ETF)?*
Exchange-traded funds (ETFs) are investment pools much like mutual funds. A fundamental distinction is that their shares are exchanged on stock exchanges (rather than purchased and sold via a single fund firm). They may charge cheaper costs as well. You may also acquire them, along with stocks and bonds, via a brokerage business.

### *The Bottom Line*
While get-rich-quick schemes occasionally may be attractive, the tried-and-true approach to generating wealth is via regular

saving and investing—and patiently allowing that money to grow over time. It's good to start small. The key thing is to start and to start early. Earn money and then save and invest it intelligently. Protect your assets with insurance, and reduce your tax exposure.

Remember, gaining money is a journey, not a destination. Celebrate your victories along the journey, and don't be disheartened by setbacks or barriers. With patience, dedication, and a clear vision of your objectives, you may achieve financial success and generate wealth in the long run.

# Chapter 8: Building Authentic Business Relationships

You can't manage a business without engaging people, and developing your company begins with building meaningful relationships with others. Whether you're creating connections with consumers, clients, suppliers, or other business leaders, you should seek to connect with them on a deeper level.

How do you demonstrate to the folks you do business with that you care?

Building true corporate connections begins with understanding the necessity of considering everyone as a person with their aspirations, motivations, and interests. The following are tactics you may utilize in developing real business partnerships.

### 1. Create A Valuable Product Or Service

Every connection begins with an introduction, and often for companies, this is the toughest step. I'm a believer in an inbound strategy. It's a lot simpler to form a connection when a visitor has found you via something important that you've produced to aid them. Play to your strengths. Do you want to capture flies with honey or do you want to rush about with a net?

## 2. Identify How You Can Provide Additional Value

Find common ground and determine how you can provide value with your time, resources, contacts, or experience. Along with having a cadence of check-ins to connect (such as setting reminders), these are all key to maintaining honest connections.

## 3. Have Excellent Customer Service

Customer service is the #1 free approach for development and connection building. Work on refining every encounter or moment of truth with your consumers to leave them as enthusiastic enthusiasts of your brand.

Advertising is no longer as potent as it once was. A referral army of fans who enjoy above-average encounters will go out of their way to build your brand.

## 4. Partner With Other Businesses

Honor your consumers and show them your appreciation—don't simply utter the words. Add value by helping them see how much you care. Additionally, promote and connect with companies that feed one another or function well together. If you offer food, recommend a local wine store! Think about companies that you adore, seek out their owners, and discover innovative methods to package themselves together because there is strength in numbers!

## 5. Focus On Mutual Success

Focus on the achievements of others and be honest. No one wants to work with someone who is in it for themselves. The finest business connections we had, occurred when we focused on mutual achievement and trust. We know that when circumstances go bad, we'll be in it together.

## 6. Build Trust And Establish Credibility

The cornerstone of connection development is trust and credibility. Authenticity is a given. At my firm, we treat every single customer and project like our own. We are fully devoted to their success, and we live the talk. If we meet a person or organization that may benefit from another link, we make an introduction. That's good old-fashioned networking. What goes around, comes around.

## 7. Focus On Relational Value, Not Transactional Value

Cultivate your network and contacts each day. Don't approach individuals in a transactional manner. Meet with them or phone periodically. Get to know their needs, values, and what motivates them. Ask yourself, "How can I be of service and value to them?" Remember, it isn't about you but about them. They will remember how you made them feel.

## 8. Treat People Like Your Friends And Family

individuals purchase from individuals they like. Treat them how you would treat your friends and family. Be yourself, be vulnerable, and demonstrate a genuine interest in the other person in addition to the commercial value that you currently give.

## 9. Put Your Customer First

Put your consumer first even if it hurts you to do so in the near term. In the long run, your consumers will remember what you did, and putting them first will pay off nicely over the long term.

## 10. Stay True To Your Business Values

Clear and consistent corporate and personal core principles help align all stakeholders, both internal and external. Being prepared to employ, fire, and lose money for your principles conveys a powerful brand promise and guarantees a shared vision. The common vision and associated values serve as the foundation of successful connections with your employees—and with the appropriate customers, prospects, and other peers.

www.ingramcontent.com/pod-product-compliance
Lightning Source LLC
Chambersburg PA
CBHW070854260726
48661CB00004B/1406